YOUR TUDOR

Homework Helper

by Alice Proctor

Consultant: Alison Howard

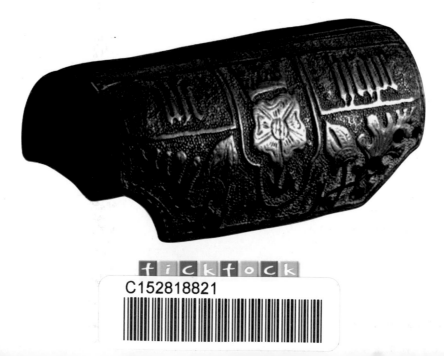

ticktock

How to use this book

Each topic in this book is clearly labelled and contains all these components:

Topic heading

Introduction to the topic

Sub-topic 1 offers complete information about one aspect of the topic

Choose a word from the Keyword Contents on page 3. Then, turn to the correct page and look for your word in BOLD CAPITALS. This will take you straight to the information you need

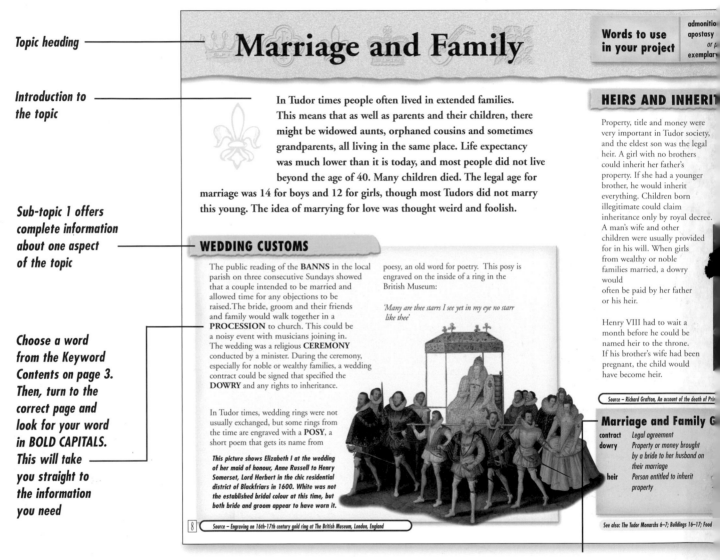

Words to use in your project
admonitio
apostasy
or p
exemplar

Marriage and Family

In Tudor times people often lived in extended families. This means that as well as parents and their children, there might be widowed aunts, orphaned cousins and sometimes grandparents, all living in the same place. Life expectancy was much lower than it is today, and most people did not live beyond the age of 40. Many children died. The legal age for marriage was 14 for boys and 12 for girls, though most Tudors did not marry this young. The idea of marrying for love was thought weird and foolish.

WEDDING CUSTOMS

The public reading of the **BANNS** in the local parish on three consecutive Sundays showed that a couple intended to be married and allowed time for any objections to be raised. The bride, groom and their friends and family would walk together in a **PROCESSION** to church. This could be a noisy event with musicians joining in. The wedding was a religious **CEREMONY** conducted by a minister. During the ceremony, especially for noble or wealthy families, a wedding contract could be signed that specified the **DOWRY** and any rights to inheritance.

In Tudor times, wedding rings were not usually exchanged, but some rings from the time are engraved with a **POSY**, a short poem that gets its name from

poesy, an old word for poetry. This posy is engraved on the inside of a ring in the British Museum:

'Many are thee starrs I see yet in my eye no starr like thee'

This picture shows Elizabeth I at the wedding of her maid of honour, Anne Russell to Henry Somerset, Lord Herbert in the chic residential district of Blackfriars in 1600. White was not the established bridal colour at this time, but both bride and groom appear to have worn it.

Source – Engraving on 16th-17th century gold ring at The British Museum, London, England

HEIRS AND INHERIT

Property, title and money were very important in Tudor society, and the eldest son was the legal heir. A girl with no brothers could inherit her father's property. If she had a younger brother, he would inherit everything. Children born illegitimate could claim inheritance only by royal decree. A man's wife and other children were usually provided for in his will. When girls from wealthy or noble families married, a dowry would often be paid by her father or his heir.

Henry VIII had to wait a month before he could be named heir to the throne. If his brother's wife had been pregnant, the child would have become heir.

Source – Richard Grafton, An account of the death of Prin

Marriage and Family G
contract	Legal agreement
dowry	Property or money brought by a bride to her husband on their marriage
heir	Person entitled to inherit property

See also: The Tudor Monarchs 6–7; Buildings 16–17; Food

The Glossary explains the meaning of any unusual or difficult words appearing on these two pages

Copyright © *ticktock* Entertainment Ltd 2006

First published in Great Britain in 2005 by *ticktock* Media Ltd.

Unit 2, Orchard Business Centre, North Farm Road, Tunbridge Wells, Kent, TN2 3XF

ISBN 1 86007 828 1 PB

Printed in Hong Kong

A CIP catalogue record for this book is available from the British Library.

Sub-topic 2 offers complete information about one aspect of the topic

Some suggested words to use in your project

The Case Study is a closer look at a famous person, artefact or building that relates to the topic

Each photo or illustration is described and discussed in its accompanying text

Captions clearly explain what is in the picture

Other pages in the book that relate to what you have read here are listed in this bar

At the bottom of some sections, a reference bar tells you where the quote has come from

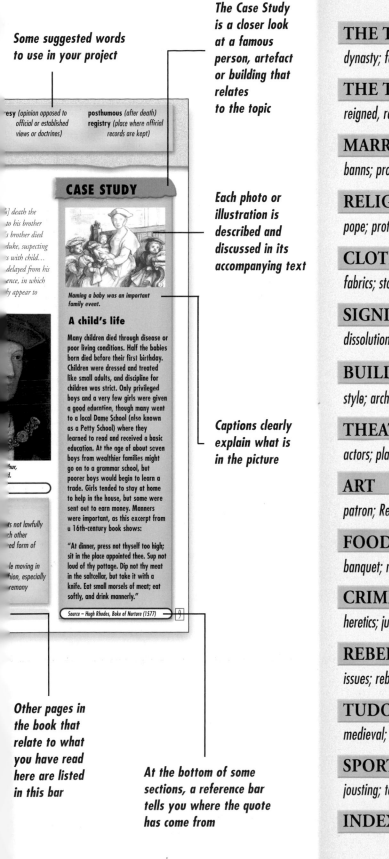

...resy (opinion opposed to official or established views or doctrines)

posthumous (after death)
registry (place where official records are kept)

CASE STUDY

Naming a baby was an important family event.

A child's life

Many children died through disease or poor living conditions. Half the babies born died before their first birthday. Children were dressed and treated like small adults, and discipline for children was strict. Only privileged boys and a very few girls were given a good education, though many went to a local Dame School (also known as a Petty School) where they learned to read and received a basic education. At the age of about seven boys from wealthier families might go on to a grammar school, but poorer boys would begin to learn a trade. Girls tended to stay at home to help in the house, but some were sent out to earn money. Manners were important, as this excerpt from a 16th-century book shows:

"At dinner, press not thyself too high; sit in the place appointed thee. Sup not loud of thy pottage. Dip not thy meat in the saltcellar, but take it with a knife. Eat small morsels of meat; eat softly, and drink mannerly."

Source – Hugh Rhodes, Boke of Nurture (1577)

Keyword Contents

The Tudors

The Tudors were a family that ruled England from 1485 to 1603. Henry Tudor became the first Tudor king, Henry VII, in 1485 when he defeated Richard III of York at the Battle of Bosworth Field. This ended a 30-year conflict known as the Wars of the Roses, and established the Tudor DYNASTY. Henry VII married Elizabeth of York to unite the two FEUDING sides. The age of the Tudors produced two of England's best-known and successful MONARCHS, Henry VIII and Elizabeth I.

THE RISE OF THE TUDORS

When Henry VII came to the throne he had to restore peace and stability to the country. He used his royal power and strong government cleverly to stop members of the nobility overthrowing him. They had private armies, so he ordered them to be disbanded and he also seized much of their wealth. Henry VII had his own bodyguard, the Yeoman of the Guard, which still exist as the famous 'Beefeaters' at the Tower of London. Soon he had established his royal authority and was strong enough to prevent any revolt. The **OBITUARY** of King Henry VII gives us an idea of his power:

'He well knew how to maintain his royal majesty and all which appertains to kingship at every time and in every place.'

The merchants and small landowners supported him and he acquired the moral support of the people of England. By the time of his death in 1509, England was the most prosperous and stable it had been for 50 years.

This portrait of Henry VII clutching the red rose of the house of Lancaster was made by Michael Sittow in c.1500.

Source – *The obituary of King Henry VII, Anglica Historia (1509)*

Words to use in your project

ambivalent *(in two minds)*
ancestry *(family descent)*
besiege *(lay siege to)*

campaign *(operations, crusade, drive, warfare)*
legitimacy *(fairness,*

lawfulness, legality)
tainted *(corrupted)*
triumphal *(in celebration)*

TUDOR ROLES

The social structure of Tudor England was **HIERARCHICAL** as the king was the most powerful figure. The Royal Court existed to serve him. This account of the coronations of Henry VIII and Katharine of Aragon shows how religious leaders, nobles and important political figures supported the king:

'According to sacred tradition and ancient custom, his grace and the queen were anointed and crowned by the archbishop of Canterbury in the presence of other prelates of the realm and the nobility and a large number of civic dignitaries.'

Society was divided into different **CLASSES**. Lords at the Royal Court held important positions, along with senior religious leaders. The lowest rank of the **NOBILITY** was **BARON**. Knights were not part of the nobility. Ordinary people ranged from peasants who worked on the land to businessmen and merchants.

Ordinary people worked the land and sold excess produce to market.

Source – Edward Hall, The coronations of Henry VIII and Katharine of Aragon (1509)

The Tudors Glossary

archbishop	*A bishop of the highest rank; who presides over an archbishopric or archdiocese*	**conflict**	*A fight*
		dignitary	*A person holding high rank or office*
baron	*A member of the nobility*	**dynasty**	*A line of hereditary rulers*
coronation	*The ceremony of the crowning of a sovereign*	**feud**	*A prolonged quarrel*

See also: Marriage and Family 8–9; Religion 10–11; Theatre 18–19; Tudor Towns 28–29

CASE STUDY

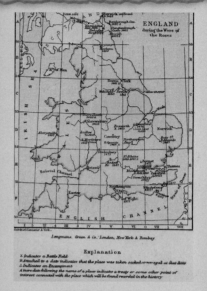

A map showing the main battlefields of the Wars of the Roses.

The Wars of the Roses

For 30 years from 1455, two families fought over who was to be king of England. Both families claimed the right to the throne. The House of Lancaster, the symbol of which was a red rose, was led by Henry Tudor, while Richard III led the House of York known by its white rose. During the Wars of the Roses there were ten major battles as well as many smaller ones.

On August 22, 1485, the two armies met near the small village of Bosworth, Leicestershire. This excerpt from *The Croyland Chronicle of 1485* describes the death of Richard III:

'King Richard… received many mortal wounds, and like a spirited and most courageous prince, fell in the battle and not in flight.'

Source – The Croyland Chronicle (1485)

The Tudor dynasty began with Henry VII in 1485. In 1509 he died and his son Henry became king. Henry VIII had six wives, but left three children. Henry's only son Edward VI was king from 1547–1553. As he was dying, Edward was persuaded to name a distant RELATIVE, Lady Jane Grey, as his successor. Jane was Queen for just nine days, until Edward's sister Mary deposed her. Mary Tudor REIGNED from 1553–1558. The last great reign of the Tudor period was that of Elizabeth I who ruled for 45 years until 1603.

HENRY VIII

Henry VIII ruled from 1509 to 1547 and is probably the most famous and colourful Tudor king. He was originally destined to be archbishop of Canterbury until Prince Arthur, his elder brother, died in 1502. Henry became king at the age of 18.

He was tall, strong, handsome and athletic as well as highly intelligent and with a passion for the arts. The English people at first **IDOLIZED** him, especially the nobility and merchants who had been heavily taxed by his father.

His 38-year reign was eventful. Henry spent much of the money his father had saved on his extravagant lifestyle. He broke from the Catholic faith and created the new Protestant Church of England in 1533, causing conflict within England and also with the mainly Catholic countries of Europe. In England he called for the monasteries and convents to be destroyed, and was the first English king to have a permanent navy. The following famous description of Henry VIII was written by the Venetian ambassador to his court in 1515:

This portrait of Henry VIII was painted in 1536 by Hans Holbein the Younger, when Henry was 45 and had lost his good looks.

'His Majesty is the handsomest potentate I ever set eyes on… He speaks French, English, and Latin, and a little Italian, plays well on the lute and harpsichord, sings from book at sight, draws the bow with greater strength than any man in England, and jousts marvellously.'

Source – A Contemporary Description of King Henry VIII written by the Venetian ambassador to his court (1515)

ELIZABETH I

Elizabeth I's reign was one of the most glorious eras of English history, often called the Golden Age. England became powerful within Europe and the arts and culture also flourished. The development of overseas trade was encouraged. Elizabeth was a **FORMIDABLE** queen. She had

been kept prisoner in the Tower of London by her elder sister Mary I. Her refusal to revert to the Catholic faith left her with many enemies. Her great political and **ORATORY** skills, and the help of powerful nobles, helped her to secure her position as queen. In 1588, Elizabeth gave this speech to troops gathered to fight the **SPANISH ARMADA**.

'I have always so behaved myself that, under God, I have placed my chiefest strength and safeguard in the loyal hearts and good-will of my subjects…I know I have the body but of a weak and feeble woman; but I have the heart and stomach of a king, and of a king of England too.'

Elizabeth never married so on her death the Tudor dynasty came to an end.

This picture shows Elizabeth I at her coronation in 1558.

Source – Elizabeth's Speech at Tilbury (1588)

The Tudor Monarchs Glossary

ambassador	*Highest ranking representative of a country.*	**monarch**	*Ruler of the nation*
dynasty	*A succession of rulers belonging to the same family*	**magnificent**	*Beautiful in a grand or stately way.*
		reign	*Period of rule*
divorce	*Formally release from a marriage.*	**revert**	*Go back*
		victory	*Final or complete supremacy in battle or war.*
execute	*Put to death.*		

See also: The Tudors 4–5; Art 20–21; Crime and Punishment 24–25; Sports and Pastimes 30–31

CASE STUDY

This is a rare miniature portrait of Anne Boleyn in her mid-twenties.

Henry VIII's six wives

Henry VIII's married his first wife, Katharine of Aragon, in 1509. She was the mother of Mary I but did not produce a male **HEIR**, so in 1533 Henry divorced her. His next wife, Anne Boleyn, gave birth to his daughter Elizabeth but was beheaded in 1536. Jane Seymour, Henry's third wife, produced his son and heir, Edward but died shortly afterwards. Henry's final three wives were Anne of Cleves (who he divorced), Catherine Howard (who was beheaded) and Catherine Parr (who outlived him).

This excerpt is from the only surviving letter from Anne Boleyn to Henry in 1526:

'The warrant of maid of honour to the queen induces me to think that your majesty has some regard for me, since it gives me means of seeing you oftener, and of assuring you by my own lips… that I am Your Majesty's very obliged and very obedient servant, without any reserve.'

Source – Letter from Anne Boleyn to Henry VIII (1526)

Marriage and Family

In Tudor times people often lived in extended families. This means that as well as parents and their children, there might be widowed aunts, orphaned cousins and sometimes grandparents, all living in the same place. Life expectancy was much lower than it is today, and most people did not live beyond the age of 40. Many children died. The legal age for marriage was 14 for boys and 12 for girls, though most Tudors did not marry this young. The idea of marrying for love was thought weird and foolish.

WEDDING CUSTOMS

The public reading of the **BANNS** in the local parish on three consecutive Sundays showed that a couple intended to be married and allowed time for any objections to be raised. The bride, groom and their friends and family would walk together in a **PROCESSION** to church. This could be a noisy event with musicians joining in. The wedding was a religious **CEREMONY** conducted by a minister. During the ceremony, especially for noble or wealthy families, a wedding contract could be signed that specified the **DOWRY** and any rights to inheritance.

In Tudor times, wedding rings were not usually exchanged, but some rings from the time are engraved with a **POSY**, a short poem that gets its name from poesy, an old word for poetry. This posy is engraved on the inside of a ring in the British Museum:

'Many are thee starrs I see yet in my eye no starr like thee'

This picture shows Elizabeth I at the wedding of her maid of honour, Anne Russell to Henry Somerset, Lord Herbert in the chic residential district of Blackfriars in 1600. White was not the established bridal colour at this time, but both bride and groom appear to have worn it.

Source – Engraving on 16th-17th century gold ring at The British Museum, London, England

Words to use in your project

admonition *(warning)*
apostasy *(abandoning a belief or principle)*
exemplary *(the best of its kind)*

heresy *(opinion opposed to official or established views or doctrines)*

posthumous *(after death)*
registry *(place where official records are kept)*

HEIRS AND INHERITANCE

Property, title and money were very important in Tudor society, and the eldest son was the legal heir. A girl with no brothers could inherit her father's property. If she had a younger brother, he would inherit everything. Children born illegitimate could claim inheritance only by royal decree. A man's wife and other children were usually provided for in his will. When girls from wealthy or noble families married, a dowry would often be paid by her father or his heir.

Henry VIII had to wait a month before he could be named heir to the throne. If his brother's wife had been pregnant, the child would have become heir.

'After his [Prince Arthur's] death the name of prince belonged to his brother the duke of York, since his brother died without issue… But the duke, suspecting that his brother's wife was with child… was by a month or more delayed from his title, name and pre-eminence, in which time the truth might easily appear to women.'

Henry VIII's brother, Prince Arthur, was heir to the throne, but died.

Source – Richard Grafton, An account of the death of Prince Arthur (1569)

Marriage and Family Glossary

contract	Legal agreement	**illegitimate**	Born of parents not lawfully married to each other
dowry	Property or money brought by a bride to her husband on their marriage	**poesy**	An old-fashioned form of poetry
heir	Person entitled to inherit property	**procession**	Group of people moving in an orderly fashion, especially as part of a ceremony

See also: The Tudor Monarchs 6–7; Buildings 16–17; Food and Drink 22–23; Rebellions 26–27

CASE STUDY

Naming a baby was an important family event.

A child's life

Many children died through disease or poor living conditions. Half the babies born died before their first birthday. Children were dressed and treated like small adults, and discipline for children was strict. Only privileged boys and a very few girls were given a good education, though many went to a local Dame School (also known as a Petty School) where they learned to read and received a basic education. At the age of about seven boys from wealthier families might go on to a grammar school, but poorer boys would begin to learn a trade. Girls tended to stay at home to help in the house, but some were sent out to earn money. Manners were important, as this excerpt from a 16th-century book shows:

"At dinner, press not thyself too high; sit in the place appointed thee. Sup not loud of thy pottage. Dip not thy meat in the saltcellar, but take it with a knife. Eat small morsels of meat; eat softly, and drink mannerly."

Source – Hugh Rhodes, Boke of Nurture (1577)

Religion

During the reign of Henry VII, most people in England followed the CATHOLIC faith. This meant that England's king or queen could be overruled on religious matters by the POPE, the spiritual head of all Catholics. The Pope had given Henry permission to marry Katharine of Aragon, who had been his dead brother's wife. When Henry VIII wanted to end the marriage, the Pope refused. Henry broke away from the Pope's control and named himself head of a new Church of England.

PROTEST AND CHANGE

The period of religious change across Europe is called the Reformation. People **CRITICISED** the behaviour of priests and monks and **PROTESTED** against the Pope's authority, which is why they were called **PROTESTANTS**. One of the main figures was a German theologian called Martin Luther. Henry did not like Protestants, and it seems unlikely that Henry wanted to renounce his Catholic faith, but he was determined to marry Anne Boleyn. Cardinal Thomas Wolsey failed to persuade the Pope to allow Henry to end his marriage, so in 1529 he was banished from court. In January 1533 Henry married the pregnant Anne Boleyn in secret. In May, Archbishop Thomas Cranmer declared Henry's marriage to Katherine null and void. The Pope was furious, and excommunicated Henry until he returned to Katherine, whom the Catholic church regarded as his lawful wife.

The summer of 1553 was a terrible time for Catholics. Many famous and noble people refused to renounce their faith. Henry saw this as treason, punishable by death. He imprisoned his Lord Chancellor Sir Thomas More because he refused to agree with Henry's actions.

In September, 1533, Anne Boleyn gave birth to a daughter, Elizabeth. Henry still did not have a male heir. In 1534, he pushed through the Act of Supremacy which made him head of the Church of England.

This painting called 'Twenty-two godly and faythfull Christians' was painted in 1563. It shows the religious prosecution of early Protestants.

Source – R. Holinshed, Chronicles (1587)

Words to use in your project

contemplation (religious or mystical meditation)
inferior (lower in quality)
monastic (relating to monks and monasteries)
paradox (a statement that sounds odd but might prove true)
salvation (deliverance from sin)
spire (steeple, cone, pinnacle)

THE ENGLISH REFORMATION

Despite Henry VIII's split with Rome, he also disagreed with and **PERSECUTED** Protestants. It was not until the reign of Elizabeth I that England truly became a Protestant nation. During the reign of Edward V, Acts of Parliament were passed that made the Catholic mass **ILLEGAL** and demanded that everyone should become Protestant. When Edward's Catholic sister Mary came to the throne, she reversed the situation. Elizabeth 1 had to tread very warily to unite England. Parliament was concerned about both the nation's religion and the royal succession, and this is Elizabeth's response:

'Hereupon have I chosen that kind of life which is most free from the troublesome Cares of this world, that I might attend the Service of God alone… But now that the publick Care of governing the Kingdom is laid upon me… I have already joyned my self in Marriage to an Husband, namely, the Kingdom of England.'

During the Reformation, most church decorations were removed by the Puritans.

Source – Speech to Parliament by Elizabeth 1 (1558)

Religion Glossary

Catholic	Member of a Christian religion with the Pope as its head	**Protestantism**	Christian religion that does not acknowledge the Pope as its head
dissolution	Act of breaking up or into parts	**reinstate**	Restore to a former condition or position
economy	The wealth of a country	**spiritual**	Relating to the human spirit or religion
monastery	A place where monks live		
persecute	Afflict or harass constantly	**upheaval**	A sudden, violent change

CASE STUDY

The ruins of Castle Acre Priory, which was surrendered to Henry VIII In 1537 when he decided to close down all monasteries.

Monasteries

In Tudor times, monasteries played a major role both in the spiritual life of the population and in the local **ECONOMY**. They owned well over a quarter of all the cultivated land in England. However, standards of behaviour among the brothers seemed to be falling. Farmers who rented land from the **MONKS** often criticised them for being greedy, while a Report on a Monastery in Lincoln (1518) says:

'The prior is frequently drunk… The brothers of the monastery, especially the older ones, play dice and other games for money.'

In 1535 Henry VIII ordered one of his leading advisers, Thomas Cromwell, to look into these allegations. After reading his report Henry decided to close down 376 monasteries. Between 1536 and 1540 he sold their land and claimed their gold and other riches for himself.

Source – A Report on a Monastery in Lincoln (1518)

11

Clothes and Jewellery

During the 118 years of the Tudor period, clothing styles changed dramatically. There were also big differences between what ordinary people wore and the clothing for wealthy people, the nobility and ROYALTY. Strict Sumptuary Laws that regulated what FABRICS could be used were introduced to make people wear cloth produced in England, and to ensure that they dressed according to their social class. Fashions were also influenced by the rest of Europe and the expanding trade in the East.

WHAT THEY WORE

In early Tudor times, women wore floor-length dresses with a tight-fitting bodice and a square neckline. Most women pulled their hair back under a hood or scarf. Men wore a shirt and stockings, with a **DOUBLET** or gown over the top. Working men might wear **BREECHES** and a tunic. The fabric used for these items depended on the wearer's place in society. Ordinary men and women wore clothes made from local homespun fabrics, like wool. A woman from a wealthier background might wear velvet, while a wealthy man's clothes could be richly patterned. Wealthy merchants caused outrage when they began to dress in the same clothes as the nobility, so laws were passed to regulate the wearing of certain fabrics. Cloth of gold and the colour purple were reserved for royalty. The punishment for disobeying these Sumptuary Laws could be a severe fine or even death. For men, the laws stated:

'None shall wear…cloth of gold or silver, or silk of purple colour…except Earls, all above that rank, and Knights of the King (and then only in their MANTLES).'

For women, the laws stated: *'None shall wear…silk or cloth mixed with or embroidered with silk, pearls, gold or silver…except… Baronesses and all above that rank.'*

The Peasant Dance, painted in 1568 by Pieter Breugel the Elder, shows what common people wore in Tudor times.

Source: Sumptuary Law of Tudor England. Read them at http://costume.dm.net/sumptuary/html. Painting in Kunsthistorisches Museum, Vienna

TUDOR FASHION

Towards the end of Henry VIII's reign it became fashionable for men to wear short trunks with knee-length breeches over their **STOCKINGS**. The tunic was padded to enhance the appearance of broad muscular shoulders and a small waist. The lace frill on the collar of early Tudor shirts developed into the **RUFF**. This was worn round the neck and at the cuffs, and its design could be an indication of status. Women also wore ruffs. Both boys and girls up to the age of about six wore dresses. Older children wore the same styles of clothes as adults.

Increasing trade in fine cloths meant that fashion became an important way for people to show their wealth. Changes in fashion across the rest of Europe also greatly affected Tudor clothes. Puritan Phillip Stubbes railed against the importance people placed on clothing in a sermon, *Anatomie of Abuses*, in 1583.

'As these gownes be of divers and sundrie colours, so are they of divers fashions, changing with the Moon, for some be of the new fashion, some of the olde, some of this fashion, and some of that…'

Clothes worn by royal men.

> Sources – William Harrison, *Description Of Elizabethan England*, from *Holinshed's Chronicles* (1577); Philip Stubbes, *Anatomie of Abuses*, from *Second Tome of Homilies* (1583)

Clothes and Jewellery Glossary

breeches	Short trousers fastened just below the knee	smallpox	Viral disease accompanied by fever and pustules
costume	Clothes in a style typical of a particular period	sumptuary	Regulating expense or extravagance
cloak	Sleeveless wrap worn over other clothes	tunic	A loose, thigh-length garment
		virgin	A person who has never had sexual intercourse
fashion	A popular trend or style		

See also: Marriage and Family 8–9; Theatre 18–19; Art 20–21; Rebellions 26–27

CASE STUDY

Make-up of the period was worn extremely thick to hide pock-marked faces. Queen Elizabeth I was famous for her ghostly complexion.

Make-up and toilette

Tudor women wore cotton of linen shifts under their dresses. This helped to keep the fabric of the main dress clean, as people did not wash themselves or their clothes very often.

Men as well as women used make-up and perfume to improve their appearance and smell. Elizabeth I was known for her heavy white face make-up. This encouraged the image she had created of herself as the Virgin Queen, and probably covered scars left by the disease smallpox. Elizabethan make-up was made with lead and mercury which are both poisonous. Again, Stubbes had a view on how women used make-up:

'…to colour their faces with certain oyles, liquors, unguents and waters made to that end, whereby they think their beautie is greatly decored.'

> Source – Philip Stubbs, *Anatomie of Abuse* (1583)

Significant People

Great men of remarkable character and vision emerged during the Tudor period. They contributed to exploration, religion, art and LITERATURE. Henry VIII encouraged artists and intellectuals from Europe, including the philosopher Erasmus, to be part of his Court and to introduce new ideas. England also produced adventurers like Sir Francis Drake and Sir Walter Raleigh, playwrights including William Shakespeare, and great STATESMEN like William Cecil, Sir Francis Walsingham and Thomas Cromwell.

GREAT LEADERS

Thomas Wolsey first served Henry VII and on Henry VIII's succession soon became his main adviser. Wolsey studied at Oxford university then became a priest. His success and the closeness to the King angered the nobility and made them his enemy. When Henry wanted to end his marriage to Katharine of Aragon, Wolsey's loyalties were divided and he eventually fell from favour. He was arrested on a charge of high **TREASON**, but died on his way to London in 1530.

In Act 4, scene 2 of Shakespeare's King Henry VIII, Katharine of Aragon describes Wolsey.

'He was a man
Of an unbounded stomach, ever ranking
Himself with princes...
His promises were, as he then was, mighty;
But his performance, as he is now, nothing...'

Sir Walter Raleigh came to Elizabeth I's attention because of his military achievements and charm. She also imprisoned him in the Tower of London for falling in love with one of her maids of honour. He was released, but his flamboyant character made him unpopular. When Elizabeth died, his enemies turned James I against him. He was eventually beheaded after the failure of an expedition to the Orinoco in search of gold. Raleigh had great courage. At his execution he asked to see the axe and said, *'This is a sharp Medicine, but it is a Physician for all Diseases.'*

Thomas Wolsey became Lord Chancellor of England.

Source – William Shakespeare, King Henry VIII (1613)

Words to use in your project

ecstatic *Elated, overjoyed*
exultant *Jubilant*
indignant *Displeased*

jurisdiction *Authority*
polemic *Debate, argument;*
recant *Renounce in a formal or*

public way
scrupulous *Extremely careful*

FAMOUS CITIZENS

Thomas Cromwell was a lawyer and a great statesman who became Henry VIII's **ADVISER** after Wolsey's death. In 1535 Henry VIII asked him to investigate allegations of corruption in English monasteries. His report led to their **DISSOLUTION** and moved England further towards becoming a Protestant nation. Cromwell persuaded Henry to marry Anne of Cleves, which was a disaster. Henry turned against him, and in 1540 he was executed for treason.

Sir Thomas More was a respected intellectual and great scholar. His vision of a place that cannot exist, **UTOPIA**, has ensured his continuing fame. But he could not accept Henry as head of the Church of England and resigned from his job of Lord Chancellor. He was tried for treason and executed. At his trial, the Attorney General said:

'Even though we should have no word or deed to charge upon you, yet we have your silence, and that is a sign of your evil intention and a sure proof of malice.'

Thomas More seated with his family.

Source – Henry VIII's attorney-general at the trial of Thomas More, 1535

Significant People Glossary

exploration *Travelling and studying unfamiliar areas*

expedition *A journey with a definite objective*

philosopher *A person who studies the nature of existence*

statesman *A respected political figure*

scholar *A person who is highly educated and knowledgeable*

treason *Treachery, disloyalty; betraying or attempting to overthrow the government*

CASE STUDY

Cast silver plaque depicting the voyage of Sir Francis Drake by Michael Mercator.

Sir Francis Drake

Sir Francis Drake was one of many brave adventurers of Elizabethan times. He was a great sailor and became the first Englishman to circumnavigate the world. He set off in the *Golden Hind* in 1577, and the trip took him and his crew three years to complete. He returned with ships full of gold and other precious **CARGO** plundered from the Spanish, as well as valuable spices.

Sir Francis Drake achieved great fame after the victory against the Spanish Armada in 1588. Elizabeth I was so overwhelmed that she issued the Armada medal with these words inscribed on it:

'God blew with His wind, and they were scattered.'

Drake died in 1596 in the West Indies, on an expedition against the Spanish.

Source – Inscription Armada medal issued by Elizabeth I in 1588

See also: The Tudors 4–5; Religion 10–11; Food and Drink 22–23; Tudor Towns 28–29

Buildings

The STYLE of house most people associate with Tudor ARCHITECTURE has a wooden frame and pale plasterwork, with the upper levels overhanging the ground floor. Many large PALACES and stately homes were also built during this time, including Hampton Court Palace, Hardwick Hall and Longleat House. During the reigns of Henry VIII and Edward VI many beautiful churches were destroyed as a result of the split from the Catholic faith, and no new churches were built to replace them.

HOUSES

For ordinary people, houses were small one-room buildings where the whole family ate and slept. There might be one or two window openings but these had no glass. The building was called a 'cob' after the mixture of mud, lime and straw it was made from, and the walls were painted in pale colours. The chimney might just be a hole in the roof. The style of house that developed during the Tudor period was made from large solid timbers, joined with wooden pegs and supported on stone **FOUNDATIONS**. The entire frame was covered in tar to protect it, then **WATTLE AND DAUB** was used to fill the gaps. The wattle was a woven mesh of wooden stakes and thin branches which was daubed with clay, mud or plaster mixed with straw. This was later painted. Houses often had a **THATCHED** roof made of reeds. Inside these houses the beams could be carved and made to look very grand, depending whether the owner was wealthy.

Houses did not have bathrooms or running water and in the 1520s the philosopher Erasmus was shocked at the hygiene in Tudor dining rooms, describing the floors:

'...of clay, strewed with rushes under which lie unmolested an ancient collection of beer, grease, fragments, bones, spittle, excrements of dogs and cats, and everything nasty.'

Central Chester is filled with Tudor architecture. This is an original Tudor building that still stands today.

Source – Extracts from writings by Erasmus, 1520s.

Words to use in your project

chimney pot (a short pipe fitted to a chimney to help smoke escape)

daub (cover or smear with plaster or grease)

estate (property, land)

memorial (monument)

sceptre (ceremonial staff held by a king or queen)

TUDOR PALACES

Wealthy and professional middle-class people would often live in small manor houses. A well-planned and laid out garden became a popular way of showing wealth and social class. The nobility continued to live in their castles, but many also had grand country houses built during this time. Often these would have dozens of bedrooms and huge glass windows to show their wealth.

Buildings also began to display the classical shapes that were becoming popular in Renaissance Europe, as William Harrison remarked in 1577:

'…if ever curious building did flourish in England, it is in these our years, wherein our workmen excell, and are in a manner comparable with old Vitruvius, Leo Baptista and Serlo.'

Longleat House, completed in 1580, is one of the best examples of high Elizabethan architecture.

Source – William Harrison, Description Of Elizabethan England (1577)

Building Glossary

architecture	The art of designing and constructing buildings	**tar**	Dark, thick flammable liquid
cob	Mixture of compressed clay and straw	**wine cellar**	A place where wine is stored
lime	a type of salt	**noteworthy**	Deserving notice or attention
thatch	A roof covering made from reeds	**secular**	Not relating to religion

CASE STUDY

The west front of Hampton Court as it is today.

Hampton Court Palace

Hampton Court Palace is situated 13 miles up the river Thames from London. There have been several different buildings on the site, including the home of Henry VII's Lord Chamberlain Sir Giles Daubeney, In 1514, six years after Sir Giles' death, the property was given to Thomas Wolsey.

Wolsey, an ambitious man, was destined to become both a Cardinal and Lord Chancellor of England. He was determined to create a home he felt suitable for a man of his status He started an enormous building project to transform the site into a palace, complete with lodgings for the king and his wife. There were also eight guest suites and 40 guest lodgings. In 1528, when Wolsey fell from favour, he was forced to hand over his palace. Henry spent another ten years rebuilding and adding to it, as well as laying out the plan for the now famous gardens. At the time the poet John Skelton wrote:

'the king's court should have the excellence… But Hampton Court hath pre-eminence!'

Source – John Skelton, 1522.

Theatre

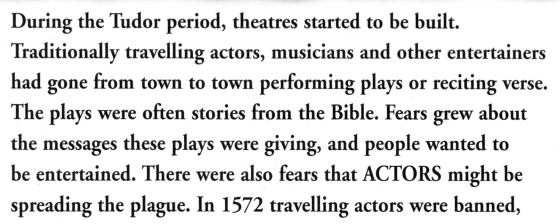

During the Tudor period, theatres started to be built. Traditionally travelling actors, musicians and other entertainers had gone from town to town performing plays or reciting verse. The plays were often stories from the Bible. Fears grew about the messages these plays were giving, and people wanted to be entertained. There were also fears that ACTORS might be spreading the plague. In 1572 travelling actors were banned, and Elizabeth I allowed four noblemen to start their own theatre companies.

DRAMAS, COSTUMES AND SETS

A **PLAYHOUSE** was very different from the theatres of today. The **AUDIENCE** sat around a central stage. Richer people sat on benches under a covered **GALLERY** while poorer people stood in the area known as the pit in front of the stage. Audiences could be **ROWDY**, especially those in the pit, and Shakespeare's **BAWDY** jokes were often intended for them. Very rich people sometimes sat on the stage with the actors.

The most popular Elizabethan plays were comedies, tragedies, historical plays and love stories. They were usually performed in the afternoon as there was no artificial light in theatres. Women were not allowed to act, so boys generally took any female parts. **COSTUME** helped the audience work out the characters' status or profession. If actors wore their costumes in the streets, high-class people complained because they felt it mocked them, and flouted the Sumptuary Laws. In 1579, Stephen Gosson wrote:

'…*the very hyrelings…under gentlemen's noses in sutes of silke…look askance over the shoulder at every man, of whom the Sunday before they begged an almes.*'

PROPS, sound effects and music all added to the spectacle of performances – for example trapdoors were used to show actors entering hell and elaborate 'beheading' scenes were performed.

Elizabethan travelling performers, in elaborate costumes.

Source – Stephen Gosson, The School of Abuse (1579)

Words to use in your project

comedy (a pleasant of humorous play, with a happy ending)
disguise (hide or obscure)
gallery (the cheapest seats in a theatre)
majestic (having or characterised by majesty)
tragedy (a serious play dealing with tragic events and with an unhappy ending)

SHAKESPEARE AND OTHERS

The most famous playwright of Tudor times was William Shakespeare, born in Stratford upon Avon, Warwickshire, in 1564. By 1592 he had begun to make a name for himself as both an actor and a playwright. His real fame started after he joined a theatre company called The Lord Chamberlain's Men in 1594. He began to perform for Elizabeth I, and to write plays such as Richard III. Here is an excerpt from the play:

'Thou offspring of the house of Lancaster The wronged heirs of York do pray for thee Good angels guard thy battle! live, and flourish!'

Other writers of the time include Francis Beaumont, Christopher Marlowe (who was famously murdered), Philip Massinger and John Webster.

This portrait of Shakespeare was painted in 1603.

Source – William Shakespeare, Richard III (1597)

Theatre Glossary

amphitheatre	Circular building with an open space surrounded by rising rows of seats
gallery	the highest balcony in a theatre, with the cheapest seats
inn	Establishment providing lodging, food and drink
playhouse	Theatre for live dramatic productions
playwright	A dramatist
props	Portable objects used in a play

CASE STUDY

The Globe Theatre

The Lord Chamberlain's Men played at one of two theatres in Blackfriars, London, the site of a 13th-century monastery. When the lease of the land ran out, the Lord Chamberlain's Men dismantled the theatre. They carried the timbers to another site on the south bank of the Thames, and used them to construct The Globe. Although The Globe looked circular, it had 20 sides. It was about 40 metres in diameter and could accommodate 3,000 **SPECTATORS**. It burned down in 1613 when a cannon was accidentally shot into its roof during a performance of Shakespeare's Henry VIII. It was rebuilt on the same site, but was pulled down after the Tudor period to make way for houses. This line from Shakespeare's play *The Tempest* seems to refer to it:

'The cloud capp'd towers, the gorgeous palaces, the solemn temples, the great globe itself.'

The Globe Theatre has now been rebuilt on its original site at Southwark, and plays are performed just as they were in Tudor times.

The reconstructed Globe Theatre.

See also: Clothes and Jewellery 12–13; Significant People 14–15; Art 20–21; Rebellions 26–27

Source – William Shakespeare, The Tempest (1611)

Art

The Arts flourished under the Tudors, not least because their reign coincided with the RENAISSANCE that swept across Europe changing the style of music, painting, sculpture and architecture. Henry VII was a CULTURED man who encouraged Italian and French artists and philosophers to visit England. They brought with them the new ideas and ways of learning. Henry VIII also made his court a lively place of artistic and intellectual activity. He was a great PATRON of the Arts.

PAINTING

During this period, painters experimented with new developments in oil paint and new techniques in **PORTRAIT** painting. The social status and role of painters changed as new patrons emerged from the nobility and the rising merchant class.

Henry VIII introduced the idea of painting royal family portraits. When English artists did not impress him, he looked to Flemish, German and Italian painters. The most notable of these was the German artist Hans Holbein, whose paintings gave new life to the portraits of Henry VIII and his court. In a letter of August 29, 1526, the great thinker Erasmus commented on the rise of Holbein's popularity:

'here the arts are freezing, so Holbein is on the way to England to pick up some coins there'.

By 1537, Holbein was Henry's court painter. His works give a vivid picture of the Tudor court.

When Elizabeth was on the throne, paintings of the monarch became increasingly elaborate. Many depicted images of power and majesty. Paintings like George Gower's Armada portrait and William Segar's Ermine portrait glorified the queen, and were part of the propaganda war against England's enemies. Another artist popular with Elizabeth was the miniaturist Nicholas Hilliard.

Self-Portrait of Hans Holbein (1542-43) at the Galleria degli Uffizi in Florence. This portrait was made with coloured chalks and pen, and heightened with gold.

Source – Letter of introduction from Erasmus to his friends in England (1526)

MUSIC

Despite the turbulent religious times, the Tudor period retained the strong tradition of English church **CHORAL** music. Tudor courts were often places of great music-making and dancing, and many **COMPOSERS** also wrote music for them. Famous composers and musicians include Thomas Byrd, Thomas Tallis, and John Dowland. Henry VIII was a talented musician and composer, and is reputed to have written the popular English song *Greensleeves*. Many of his works survive, including these lyrics:

'Alas, what shall I do for love?
For love, alas, what shall I do?
Since now so kind I do you find
To kepe you me unto. Alasse!'

Other Tudor kings and queens were skilled at the lute and Elizabeth I played the virginals (a type of harpsichord) well.

Popular **BALLADS** were often played on the bagpipes, viols and recorders, and music became an important part of Elizabethan theatre.

This gittern was gifted to Robert Dudley, Earl of Leicester by Elizabeth I.

Source – Henry VIII Manuscript, source of most of the king's lyrical works (1513).

Art Glossary

accompanist	A person who plays or sings an accompaniment	**sophisticated**	Refined and subtle
miniature	A very small painting	**technique**	Method of procedure
patronise	Sponsor or support	**virginals**	A small rectangular harpsichord
propaganda	Systematic promotion of particular ideas or doctrines	**vivid**	Bright, presenting a clear or strong picture

See also: The Tudors 4–5; Clothes and Jewellery 12–13; Theatre 18–19; Tudor Towns 28–29

CASE STUDY

The Drake Jewel by Nicholas Hilliard, 1575 is in London's V&A Museum.

Portrait painting

Portrait painting reached new heights during the Tudor period. Artists like Hans Holbein set new standards. Miniature portraits were also fashionable, and were often designed to be worn in pieces of jewellery such as a locket or ring. One notable artist was Belgian-born Levina Teerline. She painted for the courts of Henry VIII, Edward VI, Mary I and Elizabeth I from 1546 until her death in 1576.

A favourite of Elizabeth I was Nicholas Hilliard, who used a special painting technique. Here he describes how his style pleased Elizabeth.

'…for the lyne without shadows showeth all to good jugment, but the shadowe without lyne showeth nothing.'

Many famous Elizabethans sat for him including Sir Walter Raleigh and Sir Francis Drake.

Source – Nicholas Hilliard, The Arte of Limning, (1600)

Food and Drink

People in Tudor England ate better-quality food than in the rest of Europe. Often these types of event were more to do with show than eating food. Wealthier people tended to eat a lot a of meat, while the diet of ordinary people included a lot of fruit and vegetables. This was because meat was considered a luxury and vegetables were regarded as the poor man's food. Bread, butter and cheese were also eaten, and as it was safer to drink beer than water it was the standard drink for children as well as adults.

MEAT AND BREAD

Rich people ate the meat of a wide range of wild and domesticated animals including deer, boar, rabbit, sheep, cows, goat and pigs. They also ate fish and birds including peacock, goose, pigeon, blackbirds and doves. Poor people could not afford to eat meat at every meal but they sometimes enjoyed chicken, **MUTTON** or rabbit. Food left over from **BANQUETS** and **FEASTS** would be given to servants and poor people. The Tudors did not have much dietary knowledge, and rich people often suffered from diseases like scurvy. This was because they lacked the essential **VITAMINS** and **MINERALS** found in fruit and vegetables. Meat was often cooked with fruit, which made it taste sweet. This contemporary account describes the meat-eating habits of Tudor people.

'*…there is no restraint of any meat either for religious sake or public order in England, but it is lawful for every man to feed upon whatsoever he is able to purchase.*'

Bread was very different to what we have today. Only the very rich could afford white bread. This was called manchet and was made from finer and more expensive flour. Yeoman's bread was a darker colour and less expensive, while the poorer people ate dark brown or black bread known as carter's bread.

The gentry and wealthy merchants used silver spoons, flagons and cups for dining. These silver 'apostle' spoons were made in London in about 1536. The bowl of each is inscribed with the letters IHS, which represent the word 'Jesus'.

Source – William Harrison, Description Of Elizabethan England (1577)

FEASTING

Throughout the year Tudor people celebrated special days or holidays, including Shrove Tuesday, Easter and Christmas, with feasts. Christmas puddings were made of meat, oatmeal and **SPICES**. Sugar was only for the rich, so honey was used to sweeten foods and almond, cinnamon and cloves were common flavourings. The spirit of feasting is illustrated in a poem by the 16th-century poet George Wither.

'So now is come our joyful'st feast,
Let every man be jolly…
Drown sorrow in a cup of wine,
And let us all be merry.'

This painting, *Feasting (Wedding at Bermondsey)* by Joris Hoefnagel (1569) shows the food and wine on offer during Tudor celebrations.

Source – George Wither, A Christmas Carol (1633)

Food and Drink Glossary

abroad	In a foreign country or countries	**scurvy**	A vitamin deficiency characterized by weakness and spongy gums.
banquet	Ceremonial dinner	**tapioca**	A starchy, granular food used to make puddings.
domesticate	Accustom to human contact and home life		
import	Bring in goods or materials from a foreign country		

See also: Religion 10–11; Significant People 14–15; Theatre 18–19; Sports and Pastimes 30–31

CASE STUDY

Cocoa beans were introduced by explorer Christopher Columbus.

New foods

Many new foods came to Europe from the lands discovered by the great Tudor explorers and adventurers. Maize (sweet corn), potatoes, chocolate, peanuts, vanilla, tomatoes, pineapples, lima beans, peppers, tapioca and the turkey were all 'new' foods. Sir Walter Raleigh returned from an **EXPEDITION** with potatoes and grew them on his land in Ireland. William Harrison lists these new **IMPORTS**:

'Of the potato, and such venerous roots as are brought out of… the Indies to furnish up our banquets…'

Oranges and other fruits imported from abroad were expensive and therefore only eaten by the upper classes. Tomatoes or 'the apple of love' came from Mexico, though they were considered by some people to be poisonous.

Source – William Harrison, Description Of Elizabethan England (1577)

Crime and Punishment

Tudor JUSTICE was very harsh, and for many crimes the punishment was death. HERETICS, people whose religious beliefs were different from the authorised view, were burned at the stake. Even for lesser crimes, the penalty was usually some form of public humiliation. For the nobility during this period, being sent to the Tower of London meant imprisonment, perhaps torture and possibly even death. The Tudor monarchs did, however, bring about many changes that made the justice system fairer, including the creation of JUSTICES OF THE PEACE.

CRIME AND TORTURE

Crime during Tudor times can be divided into two broad categories: common crimes and **CAPITAL OFFENCES**. Common crimes included wandering in the streets in a drunken state, gossiping too freely, cheating a customer and petty theft (of a sum less than 12 pence). Those found guilty of common crimes received a punishment such as a public **WHIPPING** or time in the stocks. Capital offences were more severe crimes that carried the death penalty. Manslaughter, murder, stealing hawks, highway robbery or **WITCHCRAFT** were all capital offences. Common people were hanged for these crimes, but members of the nobility were beheaded.

The worst crime during this period was treason, plotting to overthrow the state or government. If someone was found guilty of treason, a gruesome death would follow. Edward Hall pronounced sentence on a man named John Fisher in 1535:

'John Fisher should go from thence to the place where he came from, which was the Tower of London, and from thence to be drawn through the City of London to Tyburn, there to be hanged, cut down alive, his bowels taken out of his body and burnt before him, his head cut off, and his body be divided into four parts and his head and body be set in such places as the king should assign…'

This painting, *Macbeth's Justice*, shows the public execution of criminals.

Source – William Harrison: Description Of Elizabethan England (1577).

Words to use in your project

betray *(be disloyal to one's country, cause, etc.)*
capital offence *(legally)*

decapitate *(cut off the head)*
gibbet *(structure from which bodies of criminals who had*

already been executed were hung)

LAW AND COURTS

When Henry VII became king, he passed reforms that created a centralized system which allowed appeals and also incorporated an efficient local administration. Henry created the **COURT OF REQUESTS**, which gave poor people access to free legal representation.

He passed laws to protect poor people from injustice, and punish dishonest juries. Despite later abuses, the system generally worked well. Local disputes would be heard by Justices of he Peace, but for criminal justice the most important courts were the Quarter Sessions and the Court of Assizes. Thomas Platter, who visited London in 1599, gave an account of the workings of law and court:

'Especially every quarter when the law courts sit in London and they throng from all parts of England for the terms to litigate in numerous matters which have occurred in the interim, for everything is saved up till that time; then there is a slaughtering and a hanging…'

This painting by an unknown artist shows Sir William Cecil presiding over the Court of Wards and Liveries.

Source – Excerpts from the diary of Swiss traveller Thomas Platter (1599)

Crime and Punishment Glossary

dispute	Disagreement	**mayor**	Chief administrative official of a city, town, or area
gossip	Spread rumour or talk of a personal or intimate nature		
		stocks	An instrument of punishment
manslaughter	Unlawful killing of a human being by another	**trespass**	Intrude

CASE STUDY

This extract is from a 1549 letter from King Edward VI to Justices of the Peace and Sheriffs in counties where there had been unrest.

Justices of the Peace

When Henry VII made administrative changes, he introduced new officers for the countryside. These officers were known as Justices of the Peace, and were responsible for administration in the counties. They presided over courts known as Quarter Sessions. These officers collected taxes, dealt with land disputes, gathered intelligence and awarded punishments to criminals. They were regarded as the keepers of peace in the towns and counties. This system remained in effect, largely unchanged, until 1971.

A contemporary account by Thomas Berthel says:

'Justices of peace should be good men and law full to determine felonies and trespasses committed and done agaynste the peace, and doo reasonable punyshement, accordyng to lawe and reason.'

Source – Thomas Berthel,
The Boke For A Justyce of Peace (1534)

See also: The Tudor Monarchs 6–7; Religion 10–11; Significant People 14–15; Rebellions 26–27

Rebellions

The times of the Tudors were turbulent, and there were many rebellions. Many of these were related to local ISSUES but in time some became national in character. There was also a great deal of religious turmoil caused by Henry VIII's decision to set up the Church of England. All the Tudor monarchs were very harsh on people who were involved in these rebellions, and punishments given were very severe. Often, rebels were publicly hanged because it was felt public execution would encourage others to refrain from such activity.

CAUSES OF REBELLION

Tudor monarchs gave the common people many reasons to **REBEL**. Henry VIII, in order to marry Anne Boleyn, brought many religious changes including the dissolution of the churches and monasteries. Many people who were associated with these churches and monasteries **REVOLTED** against the king.

The wool trade also became very important in Tudor England and one result was that more sheep **PASTURES** were needed to meet the growing demand. Large landowners began to make bigger pastures by enclosing the common land that was used by local people. As farming methods changed, the landowners needed fewer people to help them farm their land. This led to unrest and the most important peasant rebellion, led by Robert Kett, took place in Norfolk in 1549. Thousands of peasants ripped down the hedges and fences that had

been put up. In his *Discourse on this Realm of England*, Sir Thomas Smith wrote of the evils of the **ENCLOSURES**:

'These enclosures... make us pay dearer for our land that we occupy... where forty persons had their livings, now one man and his shepherd hath all.'

This is the gravestone of Robert Kett, leader of the peasant rebellion that took place in Norfolk in 1549.

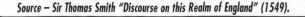
Source – Sir Thomas Smith "Discourse on this Realm of England" (1549).

THE PILGRIMAGE OF GRACE

The **PILGRIMAGE** of Grace was a rebellion that started in Lincolnshire and Yorkshire in 1536. The people were angered by Henry VIII's anti-Catholic changes. The rebels wanted the king to stop closing the monasteries, and they were also unhappy about what they felt were unjust taxes. The leader of the revolt was a lawyer called Robert Aske. At the time Edward Hall described the rebellion:

'They called this… a holy and blessed pilgrimage; they also had certain banners… whereon was painted Christ hanging on the cross...'

Eventually about 30,000 rebels representing all classes of society from the counties of northern England joined the rebellion. Henry VIII used the Duke of Norfolk to **NEGOTIATE** peace, but Henry reneged on his promises. Most of the leaders of the rebellion were brought to trial and executed. Robert Aske was burned at the stake.

This great popular movement, extended over five counties and found sympathizers all over England.

Source – Edward Hall, Chronicles (1542)

Rebellions Glossary

confession	An admission of guilt	gunpowder	An explosive powder
conspirator	A person who takes part in secretly planning an unlawful act	inheritance tax	Tax levied on a beneficiary of the property of a deceased person
contemporary	Living or happening in the same period of time	revolt	Rsing up against the government
execution	Putting to death		

See also: The Tudors 4–5; Religion 10–11; Buildings 16–17; Art 20–21

CASE STUDY

A 16th century engraving showing the killing of Anne Askew, John Lacels, John Adams and Nicolas Belenian.

Anne Askew

At the age of 15 Anne Askew had to marry Thomas Kyme. Amongst other things they disagreed on religion. Anne followed the Protestant religion, while her husband was a Catholic.

Anne left her husband to go to London where she distributed banned Protestant booklets. Her husband was ordered to take her home, but she escaped again. This time she was taken to the Tower of London and tortured to give the names of other Protestants. Here she describes in her own words what happened:

'...they did put me on the rack, because I confessed no ladies or gentlemen, to be of my opinion...the Lord Chancellor and Master Rich took pains to rack me with their own hands, till I was nearly dead... I said that I would rather die than break my faith.'

Source – Confession of Thomas Wintour. He was the part of the gunpowder conspiracy.

Tudor Towns

Life in the towns of England changed dramatically during the Tudor period because of the increased TRADE with Europe and the rest of the world. A new MERCHANT class emerged, and began to move to areas that would benefit their businesses. These places included areas near the River Thames where ships full of spices and other goods could dock. Whole towns grew as the wealth they created meant that they could employ others. The towns and cities were dirty, smelly and dangerous, with open sewers and gangs of robbers.

LIFE AROUND LONDON

London was the largest city in Tudor England, and one of the largest in Europe, though compared with today it was tiny. When Henry VII became king, the **POPULATION** was about 75,000, but by 1600 it had risen to 200,000. London was actually made up of three 'towns': the original **MEDIEVAL** area within the City walls, the town of Westminster and an area called Southwark on the south of the Thames. Many modern London suburbs were just small country villages then, and areas of today's central London were fields.

The Tudors established London as the centre for trade and government. The Thames became so busy that boats had to lift their oars so others could pass. It was a lively, bustling place with merchants and traders selling their wares on the street, often shouting loudly to advertise their produce. Craftsmen and traders specialising in certain goods often established themselves in the same street. Today all that remains is the name.

Street or area	Trade
Threadneedle Street	Tailor
Shoe Lane	Cobblers
Gutherons Lane	Goldsmiths
Thames Street	Fishmongers
Bucklesberrie	Grocers

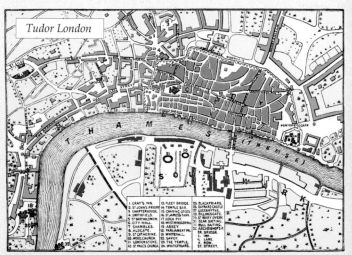

Map of the City of London, Southwark and part of Westminster. This map was drawn in 1572 and engraved by Franz Hogenberg in 1590.

Source – Excerpts from the Diary Of Swiss traveller Thomas Platter who came to London in 1599

Words to use in your project

demography (the statistical science of human populations)

entrepreneur (risk-taker, especially in business)

infrastructure (basic framework)

migrate (leave one's country and settle in another)

suburb (residential district)

MARKET AND TRADE

The wool trade had a significant effect on Tudor life, and many market towns specialised in selling sheep and their fleeces. West of London, the towns of Reading, Abingdon and Newbury were centres for the cloth trade. During the reigns of Henry VII and Henry VIII a man named John Winchombe grew rich and famous for selecting the best wool and turning it into the finest cloth which he sold at London markets. Here Thomas Platter, a traveller, gives an account of London merchants.

'They buy, sell and trade in all the corners of the globe… There are also many wealthy merchants, moneychangers and bankers in this city. Some of them sell expensive goods, while others deal only in money or wholesale goods.'

The increase in trade also meant that markets flourished throughout the country. They were often large gatherings of local craftsmen, peddlers, grain merchants, fruit sellers, fishmongers, butchers and others there to sell their produce. As well as traders there were rogues, vagabonds, quack doctors, fortune-tellers, tumblers, dancers and other entertainers.

Sir Thomas Gresham was a merchant and financier during the Tudor period.

Source – John Stowe: Survey of London 1603

Tudor Towns Glossary

brewer	Person who makes alcoholic liquor	**quack**	An untrained person who pretends to be a physician
butcher	Person who prepares and sells meat	**smith**	A person who makes or repairs metal objects
dockyard	Place where ships are built and repaired	**tavern**	A place where liquors, beer, are sold
fine	Money paid as penalty	**trade**	The buying, selling or bartering of goods
peddler	Seller of small articles		

See also: Marriage and Family 8–9; Clothes and Jewellery 12–13; Buildings 16–17; Art 20–21

CASE STUDY

The Curfew Bell

The role of the medieval **CURFEW** was to remind people to put out their fires at night, but by Tudor times the curfew had turned into a way of making sure people did not leave their homes. During this time there was no police force and no street lighting so criminals would have been able to go undetected. As well as the curfew, towns also closed city gates to protect **CITIZENS** by making sure no one could get in or out. There was so much political unrest that the Tudor monarchs did not want people to be able to meet secretly after nightfall. The curfew was sounded by the local church bell. The streets were then **PATROLLED** by night watchmen. Anyone caught outside after the curfew had been rung had to have a good reason.

This curfew bell was on the Tower of London.

Source – William Harrison: Description Of Elizabethan England (1577).

Sports and Pastimes

Tudor people enjoyed many pastimes. Laws governed the games that the common people could play. For royalty and the nobility, jousting TOURNAMENTS were favourite events and Henry VIII was an enthusiastic participant. Some popular Tudor sports, including BEAR-BAITING and COCKFIGHTING are now illegal. Rich people played REAL TENNIS, which is very different from the modern game, as well as chess and card games. Hunting, on horseback and with hawks, and gambling were also popular.

GAMES THEY PLAYED

FOOTBALL during Tudor times was often a violent game. There were no rules, not even about the number of players in a team. By 1540 it had become so dangerous that Henry VIII banned it, as many of its victims were the strong young men he needed for his army. The following account by Philip Stubbs gives us an idea of how brutal the game was:

'Football playing… may rather be called a friendly kind of fight than a play for recreation, a bloody and murthering practice than a felowly sport.'

The Tudors enjoyed various games of skill including chess, bowls, chequers, skittles and card games, as well as gambling. In 1512, Henry VIII passed a law that banned ordinary people from playing almost all sports, except **ARCHERY**. This was partly because he thought it was important that people should be fit for work, but also because he needed archers for his royal army. At Christmas time the law was relaxed so that people could enjoy themselves.

Kings and members of the nobility loved hunting and only they were allowed to hunt deer. Henry VIII could spend up to five hours out hunting. Everybody else hunted hares and rabbits. Hunting with hawks was also popular, and stealing hawks was a capital offence.

Only royals and nobles were allowed to hunt stags.

Source – Philip Stubbs The Anatomy of Abuses (1585)

ROYAL TOURNAMENTS

Only the king and members of the nobility could take part in a Tudor royal tournament. It was a sports of spectacle based on the hunting and fighting techniques of the time, such as archery and sword fighting. **JOUSTING** was the most spectacular event. Henry VIII was an accomplished jouster, but suffered a bad injury when jousting with the Duke of Surrey in 1524 as this account by George Cavendish tells:

'…the duke set forward and charged with his spear, and the king likewise unadvisedly set off towards the duke. The people, seeing the king's face bare, cried hold, hold; the duke neither saw nor heard, and whether the king remembered his visor was up or not few could tell. Alas, what sorrow was it to the people when they saw the splinters of the duke's spear strike the king's headpiece.'

The injury may have contributed to Henry's ill health after this date.

Elaborate armour was used during tournaments. This kind of equipment was too heavy for real warfare.

Source – An account written by George Cavendish, Duke of Surrey (1524)

Sports and Pastimes Glossary

armour	Covering worn to protect the body against weapons	jousting	Sport in which knights on horseback fight using lances
bear-baiting	A form of entertainment in which dogs are encouraged to torment a chained bear	lance	A long wooden shaft with a sharp, pointed metal head
gambling	Playing games of chance for money	stag	A full-grown male deer
		tournament	Sporting competition

See also: The Tudors 4–5; Religion 10–11; Significant People 14–15; Crime and Punishment 24–25

CASE STUDY

Jousting developed as a way for knights to practise fighting.

Jousting

Jousting involved trying to knock an opponent from his horse using a lance. Participants carried a shield, and they and their horses were protected with armour. Even though the lance was designed to shatter on impact, it was a dangerous sport. Splinters from the lances could blind the rider, and serious injuries could be caused by falling from a galloping horse.

Sometimes teams of challengers and defenders, dressed in spectacular armour, fought with lances and sometimes swords or axes. Points were scored for skill and grace, and jousting was also seen as a way for to impress women. In 1510 the Spanish ambassador Luis Caroz wrote:

'There are many young men who excel in this kind of warfare, but the most conspicuous among them all, the most interested in the combats is the King himself, who never omits being present at them.'

Source – Account by Luis Caroz, court ambassador (1510)

Index

TUDOR TIMELINE

1486
Henry VII (Tudor) married Elizabeth of York uniting houses of York and Lancaster.

1509
Henry VIII succeeds Henry VII as king.

1515
Thomas Wolsey, Archbishop of York, is made Lord Chancellor of England and Cardinal.

1521
Henry VIII later receives the title "Defender of the Faith" from Pope Leo X for his opposition to Luther.

1529
Henry VIII dismisses Lord Chancellor Thomas Wolsey for failing to obtain the Pope's consent to his divorce from Catherine of Aragon

1533
Henry VIII marries Anne Boleyn and is excommunicated by Pope Clement VII; New Protestant church of England created.

1553
Lady Jane Grey, queen for nine days. Her successor was Mary Tudor.

1558
Elizabeth I becomes queen. Spanish Armada sea battle takes place.

1564
William Shakespeare was born in Stratford upon Avon.

1577
Francis Drake sets off in Golden Hind.

1587
Execution of Mary Queen of Scots; England at war with Spain.

1603
Elizabeth I dies. The Tudor era comes to an end. James VI of Scotland becomes James I of England and the Stewart era begins.